Number code

Use this number code to crack the messages on the next 3 pages.

a	b	c	d	e	f	g
9	14	12	1	21	15	8

h	i	j	k	l	m	n
24	3	5	7	26	13	23

o	p	q	r	s	t	u
25	17	20	10	22	18	4

v	w	x	y	z
11	2	19	6	16

1

You should know this!

Can you crack this code? Write the words in the boxes under the numbers.

2	24	9	18

3	22

6	25	4	10

23	9	13	21

?

You should do this!

What is your mission? Crack the code to find out and write the words in the boxes under the numbers.

12	25	13	17	26	21	18	21

18	24	21

12	25	1	21	22

You should answer this!
What is your answer to this question?

1	25

6	25	4

9	12	12	21	17	18

18	24	3	22

13	3	22	22	3	25	23
							?

4

Secret postcards

These postcards have been sent from spies in different parts of the world. Unscramble the words to find out which countries they are from. The pictures are clues.

MARCIEA

SARSIU

FARACI

5

Name maze

Follow the letters in the maze to get to the secret agent. You will spell her name.

start here

6

Clown dot to dot

Starting at number 1, follow the dots to complete the picture.

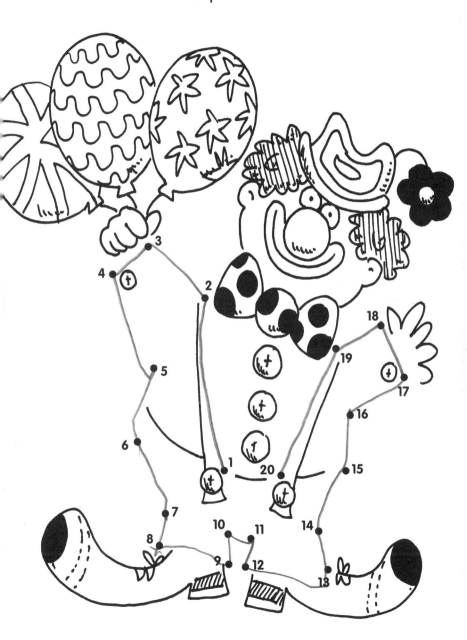

Words within words

Make words out of the ones you see here. How many can you find? Write the ones you find on the lines.

CAULIFLOWER

_____
_____
_____
_____

SWEETCORN

_____
_____
_____
_____

GRAPEFRUIT

_____
_____
_____
_____

WATERMELON

_____
_____
_____
_____

PINEAPPLE

_____
_____
_____
_____

You have this for breakfast

Follow the lines from the boxes to the triangles.
Write the letters in the new order to find
out what the word is.

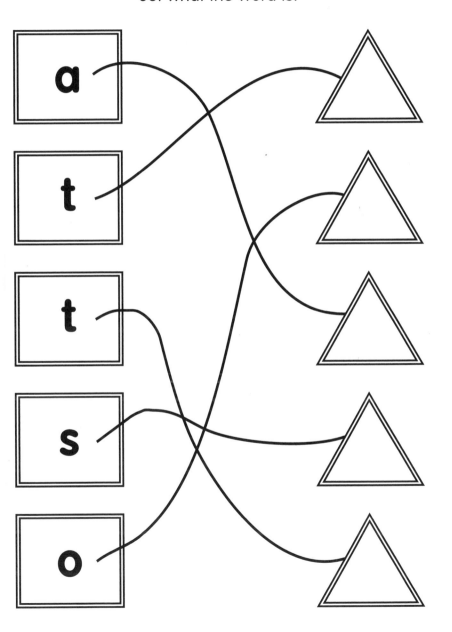

Do you know?

The questions on this page have been muddled up. See if you can match the questions to the right pictures. Write the answers on the lines.

What do you use to tell the time?

_____

What is the opposite of heavy?

_____

What is the opposite of happy?

_____

What shines in the sky at night?

_____

Which one?

One of these spies has been spotted at the supermarket. He did not have a moustache and was not wearing a hat. He wore a striped shirt, but did not have glasses. Which picture shows the right spy?

a

b

c

d

Animals crossword

The pictures are clues and the numbers show you where each word goes in the grid. Write the words in the crossword.

Something fishy

Can you crack this letter code to find out the
question? Write the answer in the box.

HO WMAN YLE GS DO

ESAN OCTO PUSH AVE?

Which octopus has the right number of legs?

Camping dot to dot

Starting at number 1, follow the dots to complete the campsite. How many tents are there?

Think about it!

Can you crack this brain teaser? Write your answer on the line.

If a red house is made of red bricks and a blue house is made of blue bricks, what is a green house made of?

_____

A flowering message!

Trace over the flowers below to find out the secret agent's favourite food.

Eye spy in the shop

List the things you can spy in this picture that begin with the letter 's'.

_____

_____

_____

_____

Fingerprints spot the difference

Shady Sam, the detective, is taking this suspect's fingerprints. Can you spot the differences between these two pictures?

Spy's wordsearch

The pictures are clues. Look for these words in the wordsearch grid. You will find them by reading across or down. Draw a ring around the words.

```
M  J  S  O  R  H  P  I  B
I  O  C  P  S  I  H  K  I
C  A  M  E  R  A  U  L  N
R  Z  Q  N  Y  T  Q  B  O
O  B  N  C  V  S  E  G  C
P  M  S  I  L  P  E  Y  U
H  X  T  L  O  Y  R  M  L
O  J  Y  W  A  B  U  O  A
N  O  T  E  P  A  D  R  R
E  K  R  A  M  Q  J  B  S
```

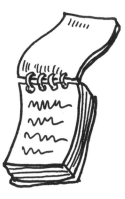

Animal code

Look at the code on this page. Use it to work out the messages on the next 3 pages.

Jungle drums

Use the code to find out which animals are hidden
in this picture.

21

Mouse menace

Where are the mice hiding their cheese?
Crack the code to find out.

Bee careful!

Crack the code to find out what the bees are making in their hive.

Sounds good!

The pictures are clues for the crossword. When you have done the crossword, unscramble the letters in the shaded parts to spell a new word.

Make one word out of two

The pictures are clues. By joining the pictures on the left to those on the right, you will make new longer words. The example will help you.

example:

Do you know?

The questions on this page have been muddled up.
See if you can match the questions to the right
pictures. Write the answers on the lines.

What is the opposite
of hot?

_____

What do you sweep
the floor with?

What is a baby
kangaroo called?

_____

_____

What is the colour of
the sky?

_____

Signpost

The spies are lost. Can you help them find their way by unscrambling the letters on the signpost?

Eye spy at the vet

List the things you can spy in this picture that begin
with the letter 't'.

_____

_____

_____

_____

In the garden wordsearch

The pictures are clues. Look for these words in the wordsearch grid. You will find them by reading across or down. Draw a ring around the words.

P	S	N	A	I	L	Q	E	R
A	D	G	H	C	E	J	K	Z
E	T	Y	D	J	A	F	N	E
S	B	W	R	I	F	K	G	K
H	P	H	U	Q	N	B	H	R
E	U	X	L	N	Q	R	S	A
D	T	I	H	E	W	X	E	M
D	V	L	Z	S	B	D	F	J
S	L	B	O	T	W	Y	G	J
U	G	C	U	K	B	I	R	D

29

At the zoo

To be a secret agent you need a good memory. Look carefully at this picture and remember what you have seen. Test yourself by answering the questions on the next page.

Test your memory

How many questions can you answer without looking back? Put the answers in the boxes.

What is the seal balancing on its nose?   1

How many birds are there?   5

How many balloons are there?   4

What is the little girl holding?   1

How many lion cubs are there?   2

Open the box

Can you crack this letter code to find out the question? Write the answer on the lines.

WHA TDAT EIS CHRIS TMASD AY?

_____

_____

On the beach

Trace over the shells to find out what these words say.

Awesome anagrams

Can you unscramble these letters to discover the secret words? The pictures are clues.

niwwod	aranko

natsdecals

lophind

34

Secret signs

Look carefully at the hand signs in this code. Use it to work out the secret messages on the next 5 pages.

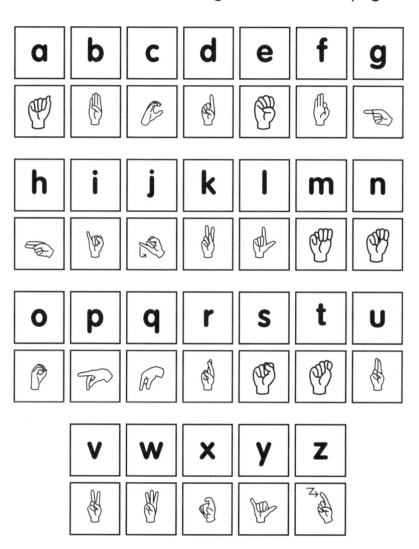

A clean cat
Can you crack the code?

At the cinema

Crack the code to find out what time the film will begin.

Dinner time!

What is a spy's favourite food?

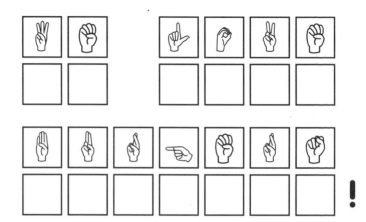

Which way?

The spies are lost. Unscramble the codes on the signpost to help them find their way.

Which way?

The spies are lost again. Unscramble the codes on the signpost to help them find their way.

Dotty robotty!

Starting at number 1, follow the dots to complete the picture of the robot.

Sums puzzle

Fill in the answers to the sums to complete the grid.

7	+	3	=	
−		−		−
	+	0	=	2
=		=		=
5	+		=	8

Which way?

The spies are lost. Can you help them find their way by unscrambling the letters on the signpost?

How many circles?

Look carefully at this picture. How many circles can you see altogether? Be careful, some are hidden.

How many squares?

Look carefully at this picture. How many squares can you see altogether? Be careful, some are hidden.

How many triangles?

Look carefully at this picture. How many triangles can you see altogether? Be careful, some are hidden.

Troublesome tunnels

Help the mole find his way out of the
underground maze.

More awesome anagrams

Can you unscramble these letters to discover secret words? The pictures are clues.

| ogd enkeln | panipleep |

| gaslesnuss |

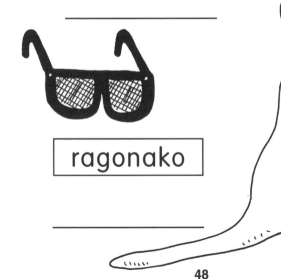

| ragonako |

48

Splish, splash

A good secret agent will be able to see what is
wrong with this picture. Can you
spot the mistakes?

Walking the dog

These dog leads have got tangled up. Which child is taking the black dog for a walk?

Treasure island

The map shows the places where pirates might have hidden their treasure, but parts of the names are missing. To find out the names fill in the missing letters.

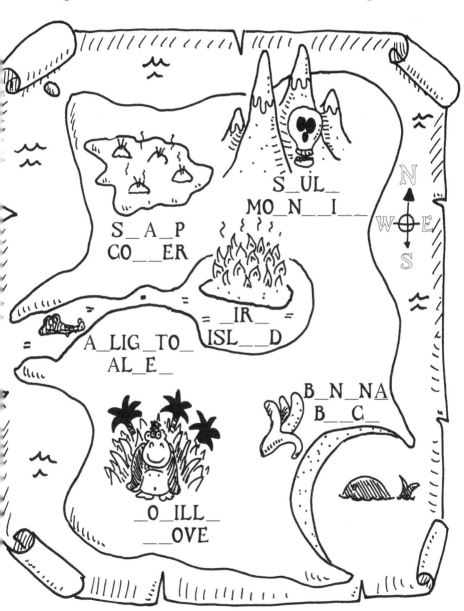

S_UL_
MO_N__I__

S_A_P
CO___ER

_IR__
ISL___D

A_LIG_TO_
AL_E_

B_N_NA
B__C_

_O_ILL_
__OVE

Pirate's code

This code will lead you to the pirates' treasure. Use it to crack the clues on the next 3 pages.

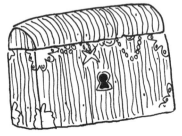

The hunt for treasure

Which way did the pirates go to bury their treasure?
Crack the code to find out.

Are they nearly there?

Where do the pirates go next?

Success!
You found the treasure...

Town maze

Can the secret agent find his way out of town?

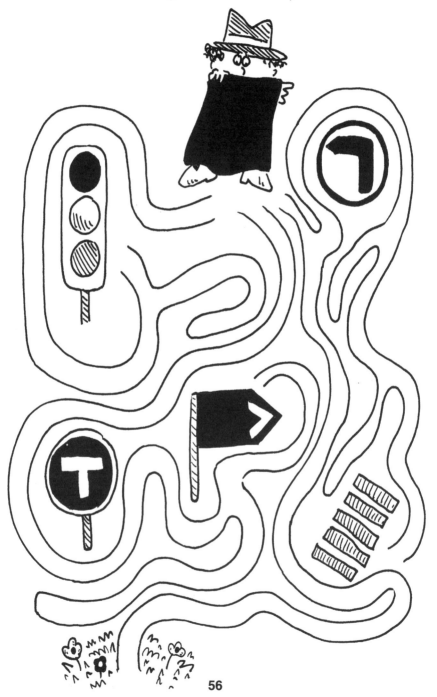

What's gone wrong?

A good secret agent will be able to see what is wrong with this picture! Can you spot the things that are wrong?

Fancy flowers

Look carefully at this picture. How many flowers can you see altogether?

Eye spy at home

List the things you can spy in this picture that begin
with the letter 'c'.

_____

_____

_____

_____

Disguises wordsearch

The pictures are clues. Look for these words in the wordsearch grid. You will find them by reading across or down. Draw a ring around the words.

M	C	A	F	H	A	T	Q	J
A	P	W	B	S	B	K	G	L
G	L	A	R	O	D	Y	L	I
N	F	Z	I	Q	C	O	A	T
I	R	G	E	G	Q	R	S	O
F	V	E	F	A	U	G	S	G
Y	R	B	C	K	H	L	E	L
I	R	L	A	S	P	D	S	A
N	Q	N	S	K	R	A	M	S
G	C	B	E	A	R	D	X	S

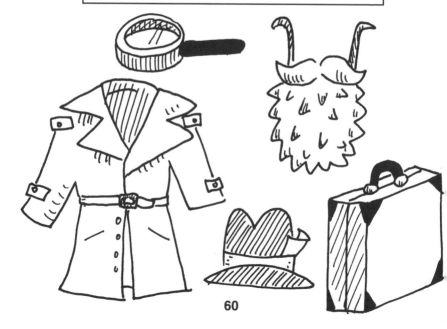

60

Tell the time

Can you crack this letter code to find out the question? Write the answer on the lines.

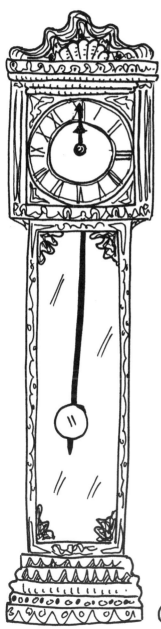

WHA TTI MEI

SMIDD AY?

_____

_____

_____

Gadgets for 004½

Secret agents need to use all sorts of special gadgets. Draw a line to match the words with the right gadget in the picture.

INVISIBLE POWDER

EXTENDABLE ARM

SECRET SUITCASE

ROCKET RUCKSACK

Safe and sound

Which of these things will help you to make your spy camp secure? Put ticks in the boxes.

Mirror message

Put a mirror along the dotted line to read the secret passwords. Write them on the lines.

··

BACKWARDS
BEARS MARK

_____

_____

Two into one does go!

The pictures are clues. By joining the pictures on the left to those on the right, you will make new longer words. The example will help you.

Morse code

Morse code can be used by flashing a torch or by 'tapping' messages in long or short taps. Use this code to crack the messages on the following pages.

a	b	c	d	e	f	g	h	i	j	k
•—	—•••	—•—•	—••	•	••—•	——•	••••	••	•———	—•—

l	m	n	o	p	q	r	s	t	u	v
•—••	——	—•	———	•——•	——•—	•—•	•••	—	••—	•••—

w	x	y	z
•——	—••—	—•——	——••

All at sea
What do you think this message says?

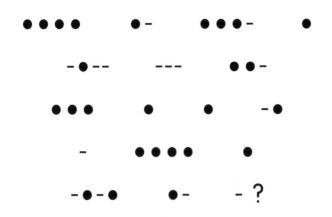

● ● ● ●　　　● –　　　● ● ● –　　　●

– ● – –　　　– – –　　　● ● –

● ● ●　　　●　　　●　　　– ●

–　　　● ● ● ●　　　●

– ● – ●　　　● –　　　– ?

Tired travellers
Can you work out this message?

Sums puzzle 2

Fill in the answers to the sums to complete the grid.

9	+	2	=	11
+		+		−
5	−	3	=	2
=		=		=
14	−	5	=	9

69

Egyptian dot to dot

Starting at number 1, follow the dots to complete
the picture.

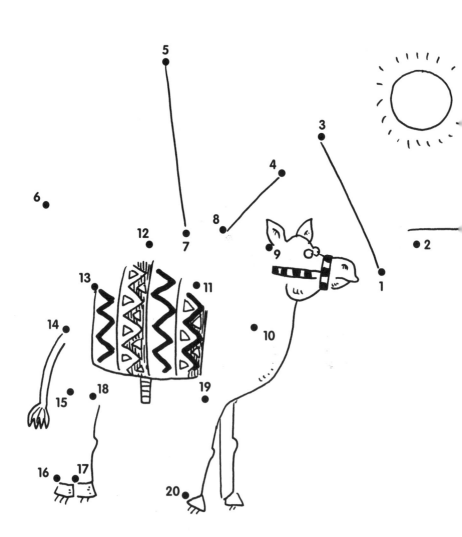

In a jam

A good secret agent will be able to see the things that are wrong with this picture. Can you spot them all?

Rings and things

This robber has stolen some jewels. Where will he hide them? Find the right arrows to follow and you'll find out.

Half and half

Spies must be good at copying. Complete the
picture by filling in the missing half.

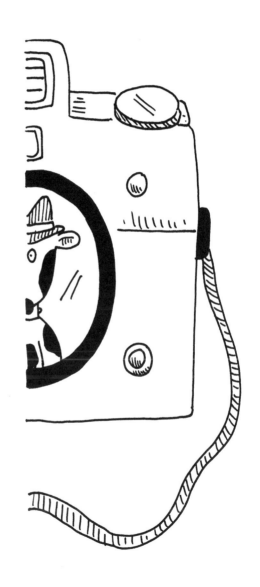

Spice cake

There are some strange things in this mixing bowl!
Look carefully and write a list of ingredients you need
to make a cake.

Eye spy at a picnic

List the things you can spy in this picture that begin with the letter 'b'.

_____

_____

_____

_____

Food wordsearch

The pictures are clues. Look for these words in the wordsearch grid. You will find them by reading across or down. Draw a ring around the words.

J	S	E	E	R	Z	U	H	M
C	K	R	A	M	E	Q	P	O
H	C	M	L	Q	J	A	M	I
E	G	G	K	E	U	Y	T	E
R	S	P	C	W	X	B	H	T
R	M	B	H	Q	R	U	L	O
I	N	V	E	T	F	R	I	P
E	I	J	E	Y	R	G	F	H
S	A	U	S	A	G	E	S	U
S	D	O	E	H	Y	R	P	Q

78

Prehistoric times

Can you crack this letter code to find out the
question? Write the answer on the lines.

WH ATIS ATYRAN NO
SAUR USR EX?

_____

_____

Faces code

Look at the code on this page. Use it to work out the messages on the next 3 pages.

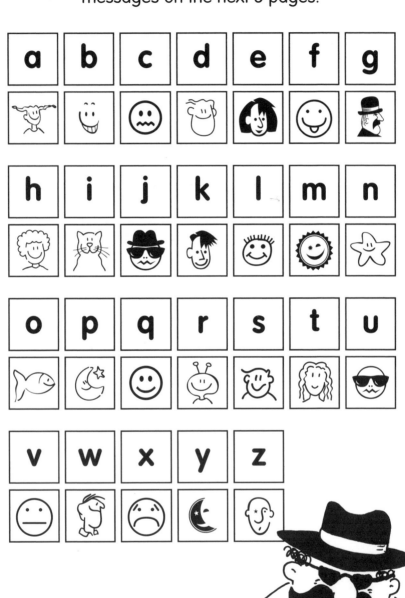

Where's the key?

Crack the code to find out where the key is.

Who's cheating?

Can you crack the code to find out which spy is cheating?

Where are they going?

Crack the codes on the departure board to find out where these people are going.

Mystery maze

Help the spy to get through the maze to the magnifying glass. On the way you will spell the name of a fruit.

Dutch dot to dot

Starting at number 1, follow the dots to complete the picture.

Do you want to know a secret?

Look at the pictures and write the first letter
of each word in the grid at the bottom of the page.
Re-arrange the letters to make a word.

Animal magic

Look carefully at the words on this page. There is the name of an animal in each word. Can you spot them? The pictures are clues.

dandelion

_____

beard

_____

cathedral

_____

giant

_____

Telephone spot the difference

These three spies are listening in to someone's telephone call. Can you spot the differences between these two pictures?

In the city crossword

The pictures are clues and the numbers show you where each word goes in the grid. Write the words in the crossword.

Pets' names

Draw a line from each animal to the name you think they should have.

Rover

Spot

Thumpy

Bubbles

Tigger

Harry

Kitten capers

Use the coded key to find out what the sentence says.

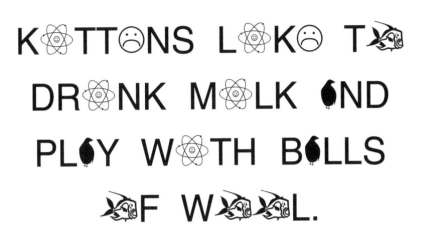

KITTENS LIKE TO
DRINK MILK AND
PLAY WITH BALLS
OF WOOL.

Key

A	=	
E	=	
I	=	
O	=	
U	=	

More awesome anagrams

Can you unscramble these letters to discover the secret words? The pictures are clues.

knodye

facesiebr

lcoekerc

kimbooret

Sums puzzle 3

Fill in the answers to the sums to complete the grid.

15	−	5	=	10
−		−		−
11	−	4	=	7
=		=		=
4	−	1	=	3

Sums code

Use this secret code to complete the sums on the next 2 pages.

Cunning code sums

Use the secret code to complete the sums. The example will help you.

example:

$$\heartsuit + \text{🚜} = 5 \qquad (1 + 4 = 5)$$

◗ − 🐸 =

_____   _____

◉ + ◭ =

_____   _____

🐈 − ☺ =

_____   _____

🐓 + 🐓 =

_____   _____

Cunning code sums
Use the secret code to complete the sums.

✻ + ⌒ =

👢 − ✹ =

Secret agent's kit

Look carefully at these things. Put a tick in the box beside the things a secret agent will need.

Eye spy at the airport

List the things you can spy in this picture that begin with the letter 'p'.

Present time!

Can you guess what is wrapped up in each parcel?
Write your answers on the lines.

_____

_____

_____

_____

Jumbled signposts

The spies are lost. Can you help them find their way by unscrambling the letters on the signpost?

Crazy clocks

Look carefully at this picture. There are 10 hidden clocks – can you spot them all?

Artist's maze
Can you help the artist to get through the maze to his paintbrushes?

Look alikes

Which 2 spies are the same? They may look alike but there is only 1 pair which is the same. Draw a line to match the pair.

Missing letters

Fill in the missing letters to complete the names of these spies.

_ A M _ S

L _ U I _ _

M _ R _ A

_ A _ K

Don't be late

Put a mirror along the dotted line to read the letters.
What does the message say? Write it on the lines.

··

∀⊥ ΜΙDD∀Y
SΡY MEE⊥ΙΝG

_____

_____

Woodland message

Trace over the stones to find out what the message says.

KEEP

TO THE

PATH

Code

Use this code to crack the messages on the next 4 pages.

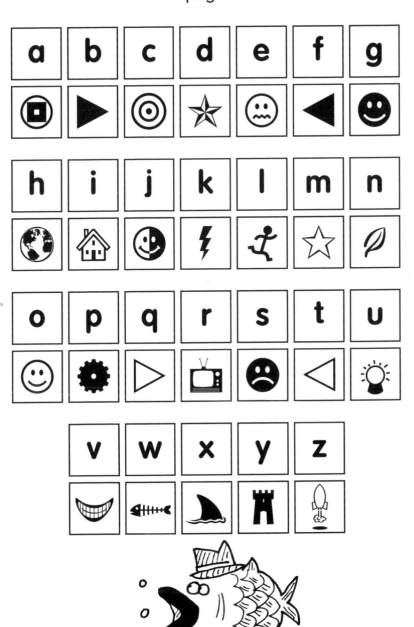

Secret meeting

Use the code to find out what this message says.

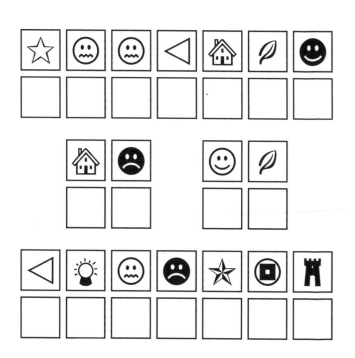

Good news!

What does the note say? Can you crack the code?

Sunshine and smiles

Can you crack the code to find out where there are lots of these?

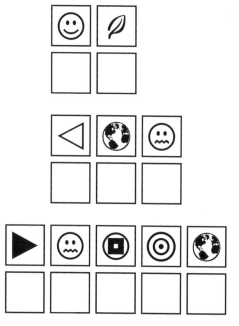

Where's the party?

Look at this party invitation. Can you find out what it says?

Library spot the difference

Susan the spy is researching a new case at the library. Can you spot the differences between these two pictures?

Shopping wordsearch

The pictures are clues. Look for these words in the wordsearch grid. You will find them by reading across or down. Draw a ring around the words.

N	M	F	H	I	R	Y	O	Y
D	E	S	H	A	M	P	O	O
R	E	N	L	P	W	Q	C	G
F	S	O	A	P	K	L	D	H
B	G	U	R	L	P	C	Z	U
U	S	F	B	E	H	H	M	R
T	R	I	Y	S	U	E	C	T
T	L	S	O	W	Q	E	R	E
E	J	H	Q	I	U	S	F	E
R	K	F	D	B	R	E	A	D

113

Spring, Summer, Autumn, Winter

Can you crack this letter code to find out the
question? Write the answer in the box.

HOWM ANY DAY SARET

HER EIN AYE AR?

Write the seasons above each picture.

Going shopping

Look carefully at this picture and remember what you have seen. Test yourself by answering the questions on the next page.

Test your memory

How many questions can you answer without looking back? Put the answers in the boxes.

How many large cakes are there?

How many loaves of bread?

What is the girl wearing on her head?

What is the baker holding?

How many animals are there?

Disguise this guy

Can you disguise this secret agent so that no one will recognise him? Copy the pictures in the panel to make your disguise.

Hunt the sweets

Look carefully at this picture. There are 12 hidden sweets – can you spot them all?

More awesome anagrams

Can you unscramble these letters to discover the secret words? The pictures are clues.

phamitosoppu	lionbursac

_____   _____

rizwad

_____

hepetolne

_____

Twice the fun

The pictures are clues for the crossword. When you have done the crossword, unscramble the letters in the shaded parts to spell a new word.

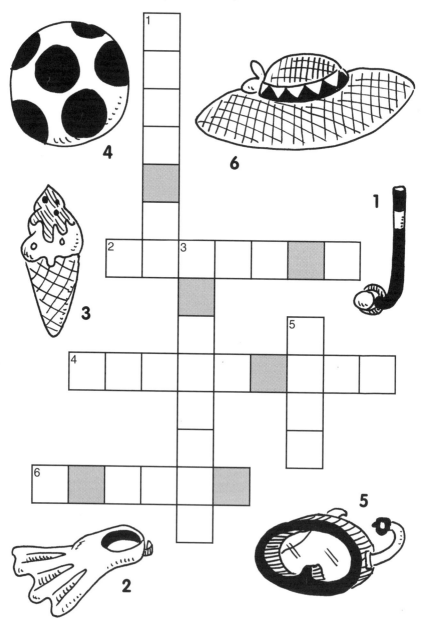

Suitable cases

Which 2 suitcases are the same? They may look alike but there is only 1 pair which is the same. Draw a line to match the pair.

Another amazing code

Use the code on this page to work out the
messages on the next 4 pages.

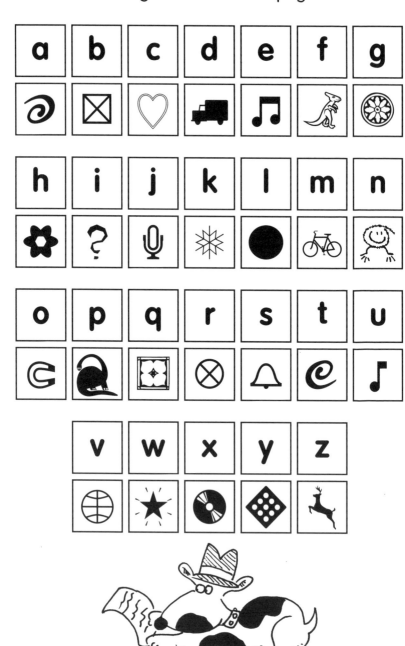

Sack race

Can you crack the code? Which spy will win the race?

Super train

Can you crack the code? Where is the train going?

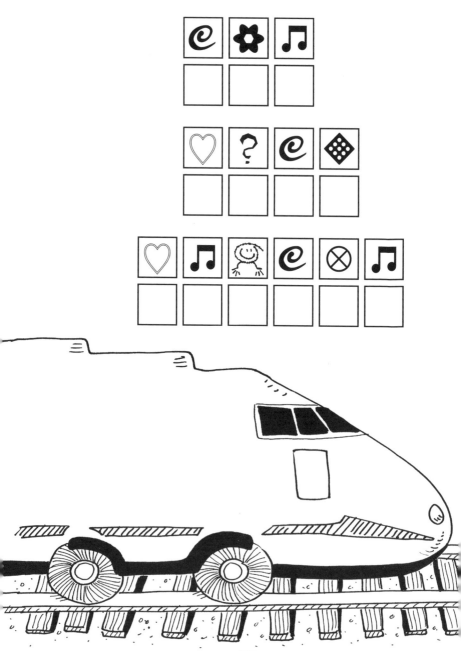

Falling leaf to base

Crack the code to find out what time of year it is in this picture.

125

In the rockpools

Crack the code to find out what the children have caught.

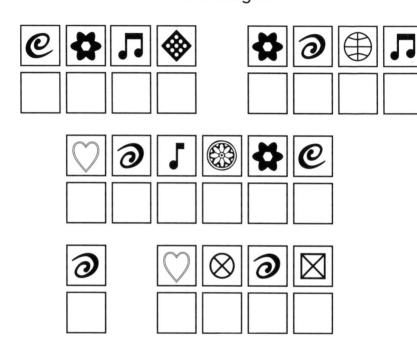

Be there!

Put a mirror along the dotted line to find out where the secret camp is.

··

THE GARDEN

THE CAMP IS IN

_____

_____

Do you know?

The questions on this page have been muddled up.
See if you can match the questions to the right
pictures. Write the answers on the lines.

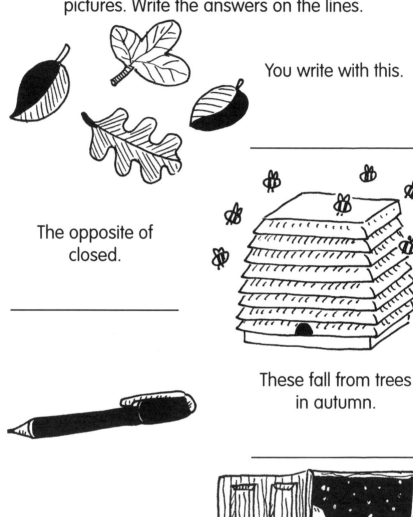

You write with this.

_____

The opposite of
closed.

_____

These fall from trees
in autumn.

_____

This is where
bees live.

_____

An amazing maze

Look carefully at the picture. How many pairs of sunglasses are hidden? How many cameras? How many magnifying glasses?

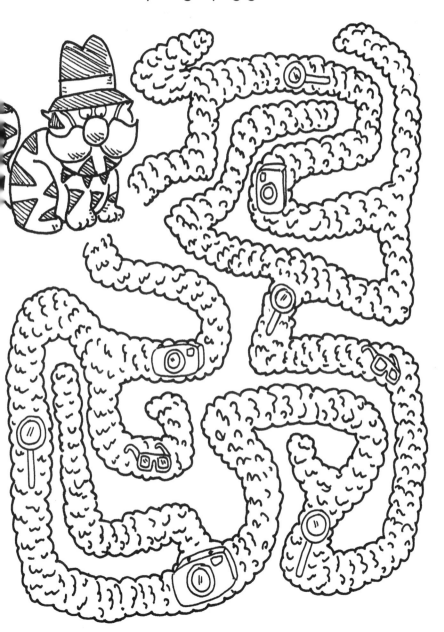

Where and when?
Use the coded key to find out what the
sentence says.

TH☺S☺ CH★LDR☺N

🐕R☺ M☺☺T★NG

△ND☺R TH☺ CL☺CK

🐕T TW🐡 🐡'CL☺CK.

Key

A = 🐕
E = ☺
I = ★
O = 🐡
U = △

130

More awesome anagrams

Can you unscramble these letters to discover the secret words? The pictures are clues.

| crumpeto | acheb labl |

——————————— ———————————

| rootiset |

———————————

| lamp reet |

———————————

Sums puzzle 4

Fill in the answers to the sums to complete the grid.

2	+		=	10
−		−		−
	+	2	=	3
=		=		=
1	+	6	=	

132

What's in the parcel?

Can you guess what is wrapped up in each parcel?
Write your answers on the lines.

_____

_____

_____

_____

On the way to Wembley

Can you crack this letter code to find out the question? Write the answer in the goal.

HOWMA NYPL AYER SI

NAFO OTBAL LTE AM?

Don't get egg on your face!

Can you crack this brain teaser? Write your answer on the line.

Which is right?
The yolk of an egg is white?
or
The yolk of an egg are white?

Under the sea crossword

The pictures are clues and the numbers show you where each word goes in the grid. Write the words in the crossword.

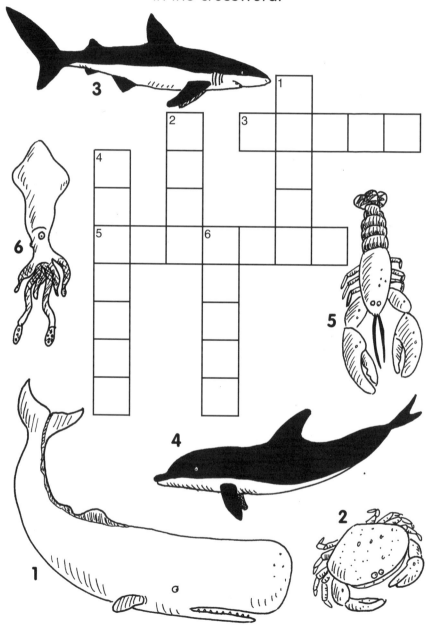

Flag code

Use this code to crack the messages on the next 2 pages.

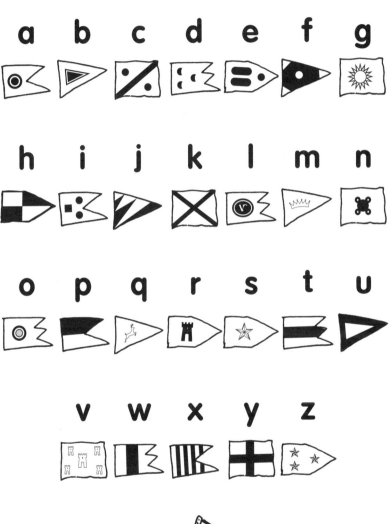

Starry night

Use the flag code to work out what this message says.

Rabbit, rabbit

Use the flag code to find out what this
message says.

Eye spy a spy

Look carefully at the picture. There are spies hidden in the picture, how many can you see? Write your answer in the box below.

In the bathroom wordsearch

The pictures are clues. Look for these words in the wordsearch grid. You will find them by reading across or down. Draw a ring around the words.

Q	B	E	A	K	E	R	J	F
V	A	G	G	I	L	J	M	N
F	T	O	I	L	E	T	J	B
R	H	F	I	Y	B	F	L	G
T	G	Y	S	H	O	W	E	R
O	T	O	P	S	F	C	U	S
W	Y	U	O	O	I	L	E	W
E	D	C	N	R	P	H	U	Q
L	Z	T	G	U	G	R	N	L
W	X	H	E	P	Y	K	S	N

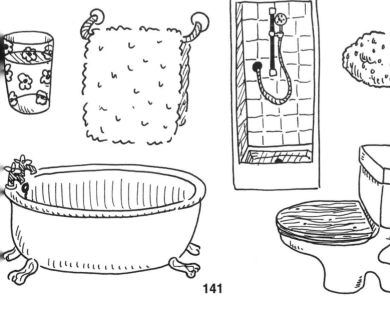

141

Sports crossword

The pictures are clues and the numbers show you where each word goes in the grid. Write the words in the crossword.

Important message

Put a mirror along the dotted line to read what the message says. Write it on the lines.

··

ALL MESSAGES

USE CODE FOR

_____

_____

Follow the arrows

Follow the arrows to find the way to the secret path.

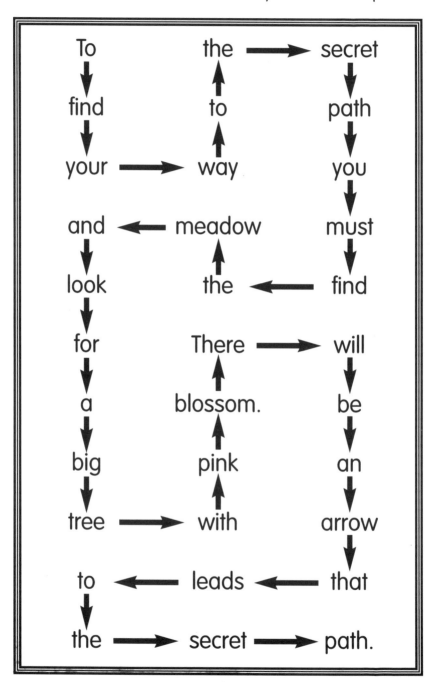

Mouse message

Trace over the mouse footprints to find out what the message says.

Get set, go!

Which driver will get through the maze to the chequered flag?

Sums Puzzle 5

Fill in the answers to the sums to complete the grid.

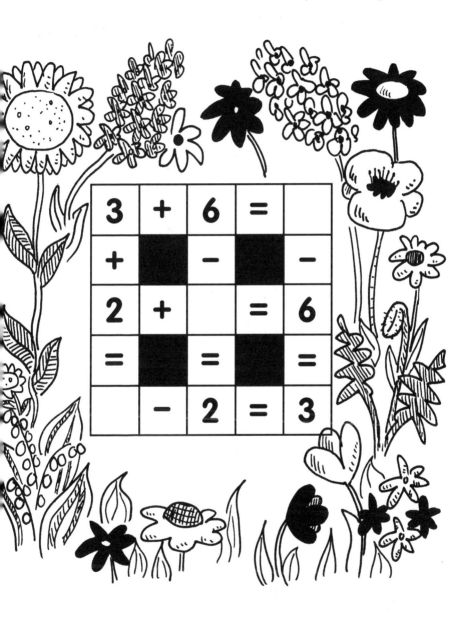

3	+	6	=	
+	■	−	■	−
2	+		=	6
=	■	=	■	=
	−	2	=	3

147

Which one?

One of these spies has been spotted at the park. The spy did not have a beard or hat and was not wearing a scarf. Do you know which spy it was?

Weather report!

The pictures are clues for the crossword. When you have done the crossword, unscramble the letters in the shaded parts to spell a new word.

Switched on!

Which 2 televisions are the same? They may look alike, but there is only 1 pair which is the same. Draw a line to match the pair.

Odd one out
Which spy is the odd one out, and why?

Answers

2   what is your name?

3   complete the codes

4   do you accept this mission?

5   AMERICA
RUSSIA
AFRICA

6   her name is Lorraine

8   CAULIFLOWER

cafe	car	cow
flower	full	life
low	lower	wafer
well		

SWEETCORN

cow	crest	nest
net	newer	rent
rot	scent	sent
set	sew	sore
stew	ten	went
wrote		

GRAPEFRUIT

ape	grape	great
gift	pat	pear
put	ripe	tape
tiger	trap	urge

WATERMELON

later	lemon	near
now	ran	team
tear	ten	term
wear		

PINEAPPLE

apple	lap	leap
pail	pan	peel
peep	plan	pine
pipe	nail	nipple
there may be more...!		

9   toast

10 A clock tells the time.
Light (feather) is the opposite of heavy.
Sad is the opposite of happy.
The moon shines in the sky at night.

11 spy a

12

13 HOW MANY LEGS DOES
AN OCTOPUS HAVE?
an octopus has 8 legs -
the one on the right
has 8 legs

14 there are 5 tents

15 a greenhouse is
made of glass

16 BISCUITS

17 spring onions,
sausages, shampoo,
soap, sugar, salt,
sandwich, squash, spy,
satsumas, salmon,
swede, sardines,
sunglasses, shoes...

18 number of fingers on
handprint
ink spilling from bottle
fingerprints on paper
button on cuff of Shady
Sam's coat
button on front of Shady
Sam's coat
strands of hair on Shady
Sam's head
ink on suspect's face

19

21 snake
lion
zebra
bird

22 under the rug

23 honey

24

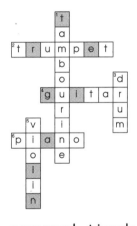

new word : triangle

25 pancake
cowboy
fireman
stepladder

26 The opposite of hot is cold (ice cream).
A baby kangaroo is called a joey.
You sweep the floor with a broom.
The colour of the sky is blue.

27 LEEDS
BATH
CARDIFF
LONDON

28 turkey, tortoise, tarantula, telephone, taps, thermometer, toad, tadpole, towel, table...

29

P	S	N	A	I	L	Q	E	R
A	D	G	H	C	E	J	K	Z
E	T	Y	D	J	A	F	N	E
S	B	W	R	I	F	K	G	K
H	P	H	U	Q	N	B	H	R
E	U	X	L	N	Q	R	S	A
D	T	I	H	E	W	X	E	M
D	V	L	Z	S	B	D	F	J
S	L	B	O	T	W	Y	G	J
U	G	C	U	K	B	I	R	D

31 seal is balancing a ball on its nose
there are 5 birds
there are 4 balloons
the girl is holding an ice cream
there are 2 lion cubs

32 WHAT DATE IS CHRISTMAS DAY?
December 25th

33 BUCKET AND SPADE

34 window
anorak
sandcastle
dolphin

36 funny place for a bath!

37 the film begins at six!

38 we love burgers!

39 ITALY
FRANCE
U.S.A
INDIA
CHINA

40 OSLO
LONDON
ROME
PERTH
PARIS

42

7	+	3	=	10
−		−		−
2	+	0	=	2
=		=		=
5	+	3	=	8

43 GLASGOW
IPSWICH
PLYMOUTH
ABERDEEN

44 there are 12 circles

45 there are 14 squares

46 there are 15 triangles

48 dog kennel
pineapple
sunglasses
kangaroo

49 penguin by steps
chair floating on water
fish in water
lady with crown in water
slide going out of water

50 the girl with the spotted
top

51 SWAMP CORNER
SKULL MOUNTAINS
FIRE ISLAND
ALLIGATOR ALLEY
BANANA BEACH
GORILLA GROVE

53 PASS SWAMP CORNER

54 ACROSS ALLIGATOR ALLEY

55 IN GORILLA GROVE

57 owl in supermarket
man walking on ceiling
man sleep–walking
woman with shoe
missing
fish in puddle on the floor

58 there are 25 flowers

59 coat, calendar, computer,
cake, crayon, curtains,
clock, cupboard, cat, cup,
cushion, cot, coat hook...

60

M	C	A	F	H	A	T	Q	J
A	P	W	B	S	B	K	G	L
G	L	A	R	O	D	Y	L	I
N	F	Z	I	Q	C	O	A	T
I	R	G	E	G	Q	R	S	O
F	V	E	F	A	U	G	S	G
Y	R	B	C	K	H	L	E	L
I	R	L	A	S	P	D	S	A
N	Q	N	S	K	R	A	M	S
G	C	B	E	A	R	D	X	S

61 WHAT TIME IS MIDDAY?
12 o'clock

63 padlock, satellite dish,
keys, video camera

64 BEARS WALK BACKWARDS

65 football
    doorbell
    starfish
    eardrum

67 have you seen the cat?

68 who has stolen the train?

69

9	+	2	=	11
+	■	+	■	−
5	−	3	=	2
=	■	=	■	=
14	−	5	=	9

71 mouse balancing ball on
    its nose
    cat driving car
    woman with steering
    wheel on back of a car
    wheel missing from car
    giraffe in car

73 10 buttons
    5 pens
    3 pockets
    4 newspapers

74 there are 10 bats

76 milk
    butter
    eggs
    flour
    sugar

77 bat, butterfly, bee, butter,
    bread, bottle, banana,
    ball, bird, basket,
    blanket, beaker, bow,
    bowl...

78

```
J  S  E  E  R  Z  U  H  M
C  K  R  A  M  E  Q  P  O
H  C  M  L  Q  J  A  M  I
E  G  G  K  E  U  Y  T  E
R  S  P  C  W  X  B  H  T
R  M  B  H  Q  R  U  L  O
I  N  V  E  T  F  R  I  P
E  I  J  E  Y  R  G  F  H
S  A  U  S  A  G  E  S  U
S  D  O  E  H  Y  R  P  Q
```

79 WHAT IS A
    TYRANNOSAURUS REX?
    a type of dinosaur

81 the key is in the tree

82 spy with glasses

83 CAIRO
    MADRID
    MILAN
    DUBLIN

84 pineapple

86 secret

87 lion
bear
cat
ant

88 cat's tail is missing
shoulder tab on spy's
raincoat is missing
lead is missing
second spy's hand
earpiece to third spy's lead
part of third spy's coat is
missing

89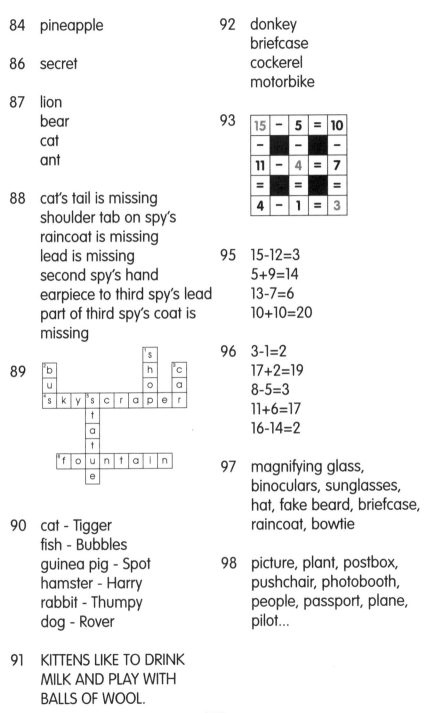

90 cat - Tigger
fish - Bubbles
guinea pig - Spot
hamster - Harry
rabbit - Thumpy
dog - Rover

91 KITTENS LIKE TO DRINK
MILK AND PLAY WITH
BALLS OF WOOL.

92 donkey
briefcase
cockerel
motorbike

93

15	–	5	=	10
–		–		–
11	–	4	=	7
=		=		=
4	–	1	=	3

95 15-12=3
5+9=14
13-7=6
10+10=20

96 3-1=2
17+2=19
8-5=3
11+6=17
16-14=2

97 magnifying glass,
binoculars, sunglasses,
hat, fake beard, briefcase,
raincoat, bowtie

98 picture, plant, postbox,
pushchair, photobooth,
people, passport, plane,
pilot...

99 sunglasses
pineapple
roller blade
duck

100 SWANSEA
BRISTOL
YORK
BRIGHTON

104 JAMES
LOUISE
MARIA
MARK

105 spy meeting at midday

106 KEEP TO THE PATH

108 meeting is on tuesday

109 school breaks up today!

110 on the beach!

111 party here today!

112 Susan's hair bunch is missing
Susan's pocket is missing
book missing on top shelf
book missing on second shelf
bird's telescope is missing
one eye is missing from behind the books
spy's hat is missing
face missing from book shelf on the right

113
```
N M F H I R Y O Y
D E S H A M P O O
R E N L P W Q C G
F S O A P K L D H
B G U R L P C Z U
U S F B E H H M R
T R I Y S U E C T
T L S O W Q E R E
E J H Q I U S F E
R K F D B R E A D
```

114 HOW MANY DAYS ARE THERE IN A YEAR?
there are 365 days in a year

116 there are 3 large cakes
there are 4 loaves of bread
the girl is wearing a hat
the baker is holding a cake
there is one animal

158

119 hippopotamus
   binoculars
   wizard
   telephone

120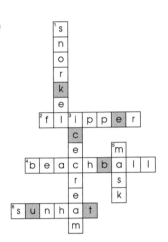

   new word : bucket

123 the one with the hat

124 the city centre

125 the season is autumn

126 they have caught a crab

127 THE CAMP IS IN THE
   GARDEN

128 You write with a pen.
   The opposite of closed is
   open.
   Leaves fall from trees in
   autumn.
   Bees live in beehives.

129 2 pairs of sunglasses
   3 cameras
   4 magnifying glasses

130 THESE CHILDREN ARE
   MEETING UNDER THE
   CLOCK AT TWO O'CLOCK

131 computer
   beach ball
   tortoise
   palm tree

132

133 kite
   rabbit
   telephone
   guitar

134 HOW MANY PLAYERS IN A
   FOOTBALL TEAM?
   there are 11 players

135 the yolk of an egg is
   yellow

136

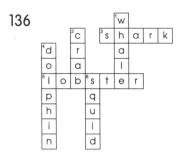

Crossword grid:
- ¹w
- ²c ³s h a r k
- ⁴d r a
- o a l
- ⁵l o b ⁶s t e r
- p q
- h u
- i i
- n d

138 the moon shines at night

139 rabbits leap in spring

140 there are 6 spies hidden

141

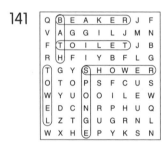

```
Q (B E A K E R) J F
V (A G G I L J M N
F (T O I L E T) J B
R (H) F I Y B F L G
(T G Y (S H O W E R)
 O  T O P S F C U S
 W  Y U O O I L E W
 E  D C N R P H U Q
 L) Z T G U G R N L
 W  X H (E) P Y K S N
```

142

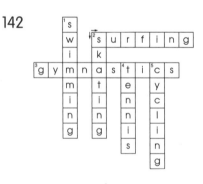

Crossword:
- ¹s
- w ↓²s u r f i n g
- i k
- ³g y m n a s t i ⁵c s
- m t e y
- i i n c
- n n n l
- g g i i
- s n
- g

143 USE CODE FOR ALL
MESSAGES

144 To find your way to the
secret path you must find
the meadow and look for
a big tree with pink
blossom. There will be an
arrow that leads to the
secret path.

145 WE LIKE CHEESE!

147

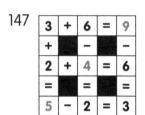

3	+	6	=	9
+		−		−
2	+	4	=	6
=		=		=
5	−	2	=	3

148 spy c

149

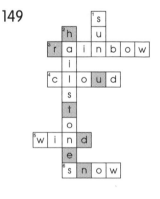

Crossword:
- ¹s
- ²h u
- ³r a i n b o w
- i
- ⁴c l o u d
- s
- t
- o
- ⁵w i n d
- e
- ⁶s n o w

new word : thunder

151 spy b is the odd one out
·because he has no hair.

160